The Little Book To be Physically Phabulous

Denisia Hockley

Contents

PREFACE

We know that the first 4 or so years of life profoundly shape our emotional and relational circuits. The last decade has seen an explosion in the field of developmental neuroscience, its intersections with attachment dynamics, and its impact on how we nurture children (the fundamental starting point of every person). Professionals like Dan Seigal and Allan Schore come to mind. Yet there is another level, we also know intuitively that every 'good enough' mother (to use Winnicott's practical term) somehow manages to come through with the goods, even if she has never read a word of Dan Seigal. The Little Book Series (in particular Your Child the Little Scientist) values developmental science that confirms the nature and shape of "good enough" nurturance BUT deviates from typical ways of teaching so as to avoid getting lost in technical detail. The Amazing Abilities of Your Magical Mind goes even further by taking cutting edge scientific thinking and presenting concepts that are both exciting and challenging to your belief system.

The Little Book
To be
Physically Phabulous

Looking and feeling good IS important to everyone whether they admit it or not! We are vain, self-critical and judgmental creatures. Weight management, energy, sleep, nutrition, smoking, alcohol and drugs in fact anything you do to, or put into your body! This includes body modifications like cosmetic surgery, nips, tucks, fills, plucks, tatts, extensions, pull ups and flatten outs; technology and medical sciences have everything we need to keep humanality and vanity going strong! And it's OK! As long as you keep your self-esteem, your sanity and above all balance!

**Moderation in all things,
Including moderation!**

This book will delve into areas that have been done to death: eating, exercise, alcohol, drugs, there are way too many books out there on these things but this *Little Book* is here to break it down to simple ways, honest facts and accepting our humanality!

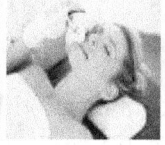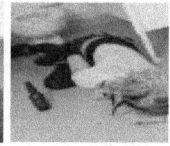

Weight issues would have to be one of the biggest money making businesses in the world today; more diet books and exercise machines than we know what to do with! And yet obesity and related illnesses are epidemic!

Clearly we are approaching it all wrong. We do not need more diets, more machines guaranteed to turn you into a supermodel in 2 minutes a day! We need re-educating!

We need to work with our 'humanality' instead of trying to overcome it. All diets work if you stick to them! Some might destroy your health but they will all take weight off. Appetite suppressants do not make you lose weight because you are not eating out of hunger! Fact is, most people in western society never stop consuming long enough to know what real hunger feels like!

Exercise programs will not work unless you enjoy them enough to make them a part of your life! Or you have bucket loads of self-discipline; much respect to those who have! Bullying yourself, or signing up to be bullied, does not produce productive long term behavior changes. Don't miss interpret this: The RIGHT personal trainer can be magic!

Drug and alcohol/substance problems are not solved by beating you up and embarrassing you into reforming from all you 'badness'! So this little book would like you to start over with a fresh mind; throw out your old ideas, fears and self-defeating beliefs:

You are not your habits, behaviors, actions: But you are responsible for the consequences so take your life back!

You CAN do anything you want if you have good enough reasons, accurate information and a supportive encouraging environment. NO MORE BULLYING, CRITICIZING AND PUNISHMENT PLEASE!!!!!!!!

How about we just find a way of living in a fun, enjoyable, healthy, holistic way that incorporates plenty of feeling good about 'you', no more extreme sacrifices and lying to yourself. But get real – some effort is needed to achieve anything you want in life:

You do have choices! If you want to be lazy, overweight, unfit and unhealthy, you are allowed, you're the boss of you!

If that's what you want give yourself permission to be whoever or whatever you want: of course once you allow yourself to be lazy, overweight, drunk etc. you might not enjoy it and you might make another choice … or not!!!

Whatever you chose make a decision that you can live with, right now the one things you are going to do is swear off putting yourself down, blaming yourself or others, give up excuses and cop-outs.

You only have to answer to you! Notice the key word is WANT! Not have to, should do and need to etc.:

Decide What You Want: Then Go For It!

You may well be on the planet for another 90 or more years so you might as well look and feel as good as you can, or want to!.

So before anyone jumps on me for giving 'professional advice' out of my field of expertise, let me say one thing very clearly. I am not a Dietician: I am not a Medical Doctor. In fact in these matters I am just a clinical psychologist who has worked (successfully) with thousands of people in terms of mental and physical health, for 18 years or more. I have been through a lot of this stuff myself (except drugs) and today I am living proof that you can decided to look good and be fit and healthy without becoming a gym junky or nutrition nut!
Not that there's anything wrong with that.

Everyone has a sensitive spot and I of course have mine. 'Age'…personally; I'm just not telling!!! It is true that it is just a number and certainly 40 or 50 today is nothing like it was 20 years ago; BUT once a person does hear the number their brain chemistry changes, they automatically integrate that knowledge with all their cognitive points of reference. We all do it. If you tell me you're 70, even though you're the epitome of youth and good looks, my mind files you in with all my mental references of 70 year olds. So I am all for not telling your age, at least until people have had the time and opportunity to get to know you for you and you can establish your personal points of reference in their heads. Even then, why be attached to, defined by and forced to identify with a label or a number?

Of course like most things it's not about other people anyway, but we are complicated imperfect animals and it is what it is! While it is cool to say you do not care what other think, fact of life is you really do!

I remember when I was 26 I was skiing and met a man who was not only skiing but doing the hard work, cross country stuff. I can still see him, this skinny old guy on antique wooden skis. He was 84 years old; now when your 26, 40 is old and 50 is ancient. So when I start to think about 'the number' I picture the 84 years old skier and I know I am not even at my half way mark yet.

In terms of dieticians, I used to be very negative about their advice, it seemed all they wanted us to do is eat from the food pyramid and have breakfast. For a long time I would have told you 'breakfast makes me fat' and if I start eating too early I will eat all day. Actually that last bit is partly true because a healthy (ish) diet consisting of several small meals a day and generally made up of the right things at the right time will make you experience 'actual' hunger! Because your metabolism is now working! That's the other thing; I used to say.. "I don't have a metabolism" (can I put a LOL in here)

Digressing: All those grown-ups who are so against people using LOL, LMAO etc. Think again. The written word can be so un-emotive; when put into the conversational style of writing, today emails and texts are regularly misconstrued. When we talk to each other we pick up visual and auditory clues that tell us when someone is being serious or flippant; so using these little 'written or cartoon emoticons/emojies' is not just kid stuff, it is actually essential in conveying meaning, emotion and humor more accurately.

OK back to your health, happiness and living clues.

There are a number of ways in which people consciously or unconsciously do things which reduce the effectiveness of therapy/exercise/nutritional changes.

- Comparing your efforts with others (you do not know how long or hard they worked to get theirs)! AND not everything they tell you is without exaggeration or omissions.

- Not listening/attending properly to advice/instructions!

- Shooting yourself in the foot before you try anything!

- Trying to start with the most difficult goal instead of respecting gradual progress!

- Dismissing value of achievements! AND wanting it yesterday!

- Hiding the evidence (that burger wrapper..),you can't hide from you, and it's nobody else's business!

Possible Reasons for not looking after your body.

It is important for you to try and pinpoint anything that may interfere with you doing what you want/need to do for you! Often the less you feel like doing something the more you really need to.

- Nothing works so there is no point in trying

- The trainer /dietician doesn't know anything

- I am willing, but I keep forgetting

- I do not have enough time, I am too busy

- I don't think I can be helped or that I can help myself

- I fear the trainer/therapist's disapproval or criticism

Cartoon used with the permission and generosity of author Myke Ashley Cooper

To achieve some of the things you want you really need to tap into the power of using your mind/brain energy: (Read Magical Mind…Warning: this book is not for single minded, inflexible people who only think in black and white).

Some of the tips in here are weight management freebies: You are already doing them but not often enough or not the best way!

One freebie in terms of losing weight is timing! something you can do without costing you any grief or deprivation and very little effort: If you are in the process of losing weight (notice I do not say 'trying') You are going to increase weight loss if you time cardio exercise for when you have not eaten for 3 hours and then wait 1 hour after exercise to eat.: NOW cardio doesn't have to mean go to the gym and 3 hours doesn't mean starve. When you wake in the morning you have been without eating for more than 3 hours, right!?: so if you go for a run OR you walk to work, all you need to do is wait an hour to eat your carb loaded breakfast and bingo- weight loss!

Muscle exercises are different though- to get the best from weights etc. you need to eat protein within 20/30 minutes after and then again in an hour: So if you are going to do a full on work out, do your cardio then your weights, then by the time you eat your protein for your muscles the time will work out well. It's not complicated really but it is effective so process what I just told you and factor it into your lifestyle.

And yes there is a lot of conflicting information and advice: generally speaking most of it will be somewhat correct within the whole context of the information. I'm giving you the highlights but by all means research it further. Serious body builders and athletes have different regimes and methods than us mere mortals use or need. Remember this book employs the K.I.S.S principle.

The purpose of breathing is to bring vitality and oxygen into our blood stream. But there are also many other crucial aspects in breathing, such as assisting the heart's pumping action, the flow of endocrine hormonal emission from the organs as well as the movement of the cerebral spinal fluid in the spinal cord.'   - Sat Chuen Hon, 'The Tao of Breath' (so practice breathing **properly)**

SLEEP

Most people have issues at some time and your quality (not quantity) of sleep can make or break you!

You have access to a really good sleep CD, USE IT! IT WORKS! It has a build-up effect, so use it regularly (www.littlebookseries.us & Amazon)
Try to have a routine (do the best you can, given your life circumstances)

Go to bed when you are sleepy

Do not nap during the day (10 minute power naps (meditation) are OK)

Try and get up the same time each day (even on weekends)

Try to keep bed for sleeping and sex!

If possible avoid watching TV and studying in bed. We want your mind to associate bed with a cue to "go to sleep now". Having said that a lot of us (esp. me) love to watch

TV in bed: if you don't have any sleep issues then it's all good! (If it's not broken then.....)

AVOID CAFFEINE: That's coffee, coke, etc...It does keep you awake, so work out what time you have to stop having caffeine if you are to sleep that night.

Alcohol and drugs make you sleep in the short term, BUT it isn't the right sort of sleep and it may make your ongoing sleep problem worse.

THE SAME with sleeping pills, they can be a great short-term fix, or a means to catch up on some sleep, but in the LONG-TERM you need some SLEEP SKILLS (quality of drug induced sleep is not as good as natural sleep)

Lying in bed WORRYING stimulates your mind and keeps you awake SO if you can't put it out of your mind – write it down for attention tomorrow. Then put something else in your mind – like music, or your sleep CD

Use your problem solving techniques before bed time so that you can tell yourself you have a plan to deal with those concerns...

Obviously if you haven't used any energy during the day you won't be tired... (Physical exhaustion tends to give you sleep where mental fatigue will keep you awake)

EXERCISE during the day will help you sleep, not too close to bedtime though (it may not happen overnight but it WILL happen).

We are looking for balance, moderation and a routine you can live with!

Eat regularly and avoid large meals before bed time. Carbs give you energy so you need them to start your day. Protein restores and repairs while you sleep. Indigestion OR empty tummy noises will keep you awake... So a light snake before bed is fine if you need it. Listen to your body!

Make sure your bedroom is dark, quiet, and have the TV off when it's time to go to sleep (I know people who leave it on all night; not good for lots of reasons)

A hot drink (especially MILK) before bed DOES help

Or a hot bath before bed.

Don't put yourself in a position where you are looking at the clock all night, if need be get rid of it or cover it up.

Research indicates that smoking weed/pot/THC (whatever) damages your hypothalamus! The younger you are when you start using, the worse the damage potential)

NOTE TO PARENTS :(This is repeated in a few of my books because it is so important!)

When you are going off at Mr. 2 yr. old for not going to sleep on demand- ask yourself how easy it is to do that!!!!! Be Fair!

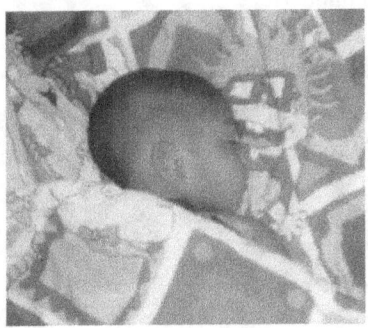

Human sleep patterns: (Next bit is for those who like explanations. I generally don't put the technical stuff in these books).

Our sleep patterns are intimately related to the natural world. The planet turns on its axis once every twenty-four hours, giving us cycles of light and darkness, and living organisms seem to cycle with it, as seen in diurnal changes known as circadian rhythms.

These rhythms show up in daily fluctuations in the release of neurotransmitters in the brain and nervous system and in the biochemistry of all our cells. We have these basic planetary rhythms built into our systems. The so-called 'biological clock' is controlled by the hypothalamus (lumpy bit in brain), which regulates our sleep/wake cycle and can be disrupted by air travel, working shifts, stress, and some lifestyles.

Physical Symptoms of poor sleep habits can include (highly unlikely you would get more than a few of these at any given time: If you do then you really need to see your doctor) -

- Pounding heart
- Cold hands/feet
- Sweating
- Nausea
- Diarrhea
- Constipation
- Back pain
- Digestive difficulties
- Headaches
- Irregular breathing
- Fatigue

- Tension
- Voice/hand tremors
- Dry mouth
- Dizziness
- Impaired immune system
- Shortness of breath
- High blood pressure
- Vague aches/pains
- Difficulty breathing through nostrils

Psychological Symptoms can include

- Depression
- Boredom
- Nightmares
- Confusion
- Helplessness
- Tearfulness
- Dissociation
- Lethargy
- Anxiety
- Paranoia
- Nervousness
- Impaired focus
- Negativity

Behavioral Symptoms can include

- Fidgeting
- Smoking
- Substance abuse
- Reliance on medication
- Impulsiveness

- Defensiveness
- Disorganization
- Eating disorders
- Decreased sex drive
- Aggression
- Clumsiness
- Inflexibility
- Cynicism
- Impaired efficiency
- Decline in performance
- Nagging
- Poor self-care
- Withdrawal from supportive relationship!

All these just from crappy sleep

'We cycle with the planet, and our sleep pattern reflects this connection. When it is disrupted, it takes us some time to readjust, to get back to our normal pattern.'

Jon Kabat-Zinn, *'Full Catastrophe Living'*

OK still on the technical stuff but hang in there, this is really important to know if you have sleep issue (including sleeping with someone who does)

Melatonin is produced by a pea-sized gland at the base of the brain called the pineal gland. It is the hormone that causes sleepiness and sound sleep. Darkness is one of the main triggers for melatonin production to increase, causing the body to start slowing down in preparation for sleep. (You can buy Melatonin supplements; useful short term but still pills)

Light entering the eye through the retina causes melatonin production to reduce, causing the body to awaken. The pineal gland's capacity to keep up the production of melatonin declines with age.

Sleep Patterns A one-and-a-half-hour cycle, (approximately, it may differ slightly with individual people and circumstances) produces altered states of awareness naturally and rhythmically throughout the day and night. Each cycle lasts twenty minutes and seems to be the natural healing state of the mind and body.

These cycles provide a natural 'time out' when conscious awareness is toned down. We need to learn to recognize this rhythm in ourselves and flow with it. This is also relevant when you are trying to study or pay attention. Meditation in any of its forms is going to help with this.

An electroencephalogram (EEG, we talk about this in Magical Mind) displays wavy lines during this stage – fairly regular, small undulations; Drowsiness dominates; a light phase, lasting approximately five minutes, In this stage you can be awakened by a sharp sound, all muscles slightly relax, your eyes slowly roll back and forth, not REM (Rapid Eye Movement – eyes jerking back and forth under closed eyelids).Your thinking is less logical. Your dreams are remembered if you awaken.

In the next stage it is a little harder to wake up, different brain waves appear regularly and last two to three seconds, at this time there can be big changes in the processing of sensory information in the brain; most sleep talking and teeth-grinding takes place during this stage After another five to ten minutes you slip into moderately deep sleep. It is now difficult to wake. Some Delta waves; larger, more regular waves – come into play. Theta waves, are still occurring, Delta waves become increasingly dominant slow wave sleep (heavy delta). The deepest level of sleep.

You are now extremely difficult to wake up, all sleepwalking**, bedwetting, and night terrors** occur during this stage. Your heartbeat and breathing are regular. The **growth hormone is released**. Blood cells and body tissue rebuild, especially your skin. Energy levels are slowly restored. There is no conscious thought. Some dreaming, but you will have no memory of it if woken up.

In case you're a bit confused, remember I said that brain waves can also operate concurrently etc. etc. but for the purpose of the main Brainwave Section (RAS, Alpha etc.) I need you to keep it simple. It is not a contradiction though, ok.

NOTE: Artificial sedatives and alcohol significantly decrease REM sleep

Chronic insomnia may develop slowly or as a result of a long lasting emotional, chemical or physical situation that has not been resolved.
Alcohol is a central nervous system depressant, alcohol may send you to sleep quickly but your sleep does not reach the deeper delta levels and you are likely to wake in the early hours, or sleep fitfully.

Nicotine is another stimulant; it raises blood pressure, alters breathing, and triggers adrenaline (which also interferes with digestion). Prescribed medication/ chemicals often cause sleep disturbance. Always check with a doctor (or 2) before changing or ceasing to use medications. Excesses of starch, salt, sugar: can keep you awake

SO LETS TALK ABOUT EATING:

 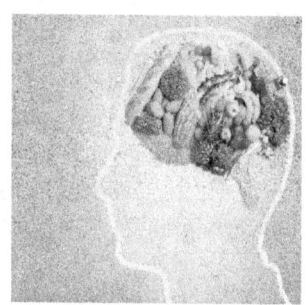

This statement is not for people with eating disorders; but the truth is …. Being big and beautiful is not OK if you're going to end up with diabetes, heart disease or any other form of being unfit and unhealthy. So for those with a genuine need/want to 'manage' their weight here is a little weight management psychology!

Weight Management Plan

Amount you are **going to** lose…………..Weight **you will** then be……….Date you **will be** that weight ………

An example might be 15 kg OR 40 pounds over 18 months: Too long you say! Not if it's the last time you're going to need to do this!

People who lose a truck load of weight overnight tend to do it often. So this time take a bit longer, do it once, and live life at the same time!

Rules: Weigh yourself every 2 weeks REMEMBER scales only give a rough idea of your weight: Sometimes you have lost weight and it seems to take a while to register on the scales. Sometimes you may have gained and it doesn't show up: **SO as long as you know you have stuck to the plan do not be intimidated by what the scales say you weigh:** (what is currently in your tummy or bowel is being weighed as well as the big glass of water you just had)

FACTOR *LIVING* INTO YOUR PLAN! Between now and ……… (Date you reach goal weight) you will have dinner out, go to a family function or just have a treat, this is not meant to be torture! If you are a chocoholic don't make stupid promises to yourself like you are giving it up forever! (This type of '*oholic* not to be generalized to alcohol or substances though)

Get a carb, fat and protein counter/book, one that has brands, take out, etc. Do not be fanatic but DO know what is in what you are putting in your mouth. Most packaged food and treats have the carbs/fats /proteins count on the pack/can etc. I tend to find that when this print is really really tiny it means the item is heavy on the fattening/unhealthy stuff!

As you go through the day keep track of what goes in your mouth. Again: scribble a note don't fret and go OCD on the whole thing. Remember that we have factored mistakes, life and occasional indulgence into our program.

Ultimately knowing your carbs fats and proteins will help you develop an eating lifestyle that you can use to increase your metabolism, energy and overall health for the rest of your life. You will be amazed at how many treat-like foods are on your side. Who doesn't like chocolate dipped strawberries?

Overweight people often claim that they eat very little…

It is very possibly true! If all you had today is a hamburger, a block of chocolate and a bottle of coke you would have had very little 'food' but a lot of calories and carbohydrates and nothing to help your energy or metabolism.

Sometimes two food items that look the same can have very different food values. 1 protein bar might have 5 carbs while another that looks about the same has 48 carbs! READ THE FINE PRINT! A good balanced eating plan with the right amount of carbs, proteins and good fats will actually give you way more food to eat. There are some protein bars that taste the same, if not better, than snickers and caramel chews, etc. etc.; great for us chocoholics! (freebie)

REMEMBER: When you feel you are not losing quick enough or you have reached a plateau remind yourself that you will be .... (Weight) on .... date.
Because overall you know you are staying with the program. Remember it is not meant to be torture or punishment! Just because it doesn't hurt does not mean it won't work.

It seems like we have set a really long time for you to reach your goal weight BUT how long have you had the weight problem? How many times have you lost it and put in on? So taking X months to lose it, finally, without the pain, is really not so bad is it! During that time you will be getting slimmer and healthier (I notice a weight management as on TV now that calls this the 'During', I like that) but remember you will also be getting on with life and not being obsessed with silly diets.

This is a really good tip for you and your brain: DO NOT THINK OF IT AS COUNTING CALORIES/ CARBS:

Think of it as a bank account: If your budget is 120 dollars a day (1 dollar= 1 token =1 carb) If you spend 60 carbs on one small can of soft drink you may decide to re-think that; get the low carb diet drink and spend those 60 tokens on something of more value. After a while you will look at a treat that is going to cost you 45 tokens and you may think of all the other food you can get for that amount of credit... Your choice!

When I'm going to spend 60 carbs on one treat it has to be something good! Just changing the language and the currency IS going to help!

Exercise: Think about exercise as unrelated to weight loss because when you look at how many calories you lose for an hour on the treadmill it doesn't seem worth it. SO exercise is about improving health, metabolism, mood, brain functioning etc.: AND you may think you do not like 'exercise' but there are ways you 'move your body' that are exercise.

i.e.; playing darts can be exercise for your arms, pool can work on your posture and calf muscles, dancing and sexual activities are excellent forms of exercise.

There will be some things you like that constitute exercise just think about it.

When you do have a treat: Have quality rather than quantity: Sit down with it and give it your full attention so you enjoy every bit of it.

Golden Rule: YOU ARE NOT ALLOWED TO FEEL GUILTY ABOUT HAVING IT (if you can't enjoy it without the guilt then don't have it!) Absolutely No side dish of guilt!

AGAIN once you develop some motivation and enthusiasm a personal trainer can really help you with refining exercise techniques. BUT get yourself warmed up psychologically first... most trainers want to push you and this is good when you are ready and when you are able to be assertive and communicate with your trainer: FYI: Most people forget that, whether it's your doctor, therapist, agent or trainer; they are working for you, your staff! NOT authoritarian figures, NOT the boss of you!

GIVE UP ONE THING: It may be bread or butter... (or both)...something in your usual eating habits that is substantial in terms of carbs/calories (You can change this every 3 or 6 months if you wish).

ALSO....YOU ALREADY KNOW you need to put up smaller servings BUT you also need to do this:-
AS SOON AS YOU FEEL A SLIGHT FULLNESS PUT YOUR FOOD DOWN!!!!

YOU CAN STILL EAT IT BUT PUT IT DOWN FOR A FEW MINUTES, GO GET A DRINK OF WATER OR DO SOMETHING: YOU CAN THEN COME BACK AND FINISH YOUR FOOD (MOST STUFF TASTES GOOD COLD-IF IT IS NOT THAT YUMMY FOOD WHY EAT MORE ANYWAY).

Don't be surprised though, if you lose interest in it and throw it out or put it away for later! You **can** throw good food in the bin... you already bought it and cooked it. The starving kids in Africa will not be affected differently by whether you put in the bin or on your butt.

The more you can learn to have frequents small meals the sooner your energy and metabolism will get going: every 2/3 hours is good and try to keep your carbs for earlier in the day when you need energy and your proteins for later so that they can build and repair your body while you sleep. (Again athletes will have variations on this, their body and its requirements are not the same as yours). Oh, and if you *were* an athlete 10 years ago you do not want to eat the same way now!

MOST IMPORTANT IS POSITIVE REINFORCEMENT, ENCOURAGEMENT & BEING PROUD OF THE SLIGHTEST ACHIEVEMENT. YOU WILL ALWAYS BE DRAWN TO REWARDING SITUATIONS AND RUN FROM PUNISHING EVENTS.

Cosmetic Enhancements, Vanity & Aesthetics

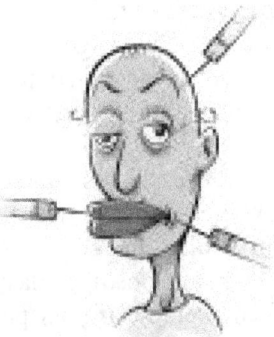

I'm going to touch briefly on nips, tucks, sucks and fillers. All the tricks and products available to us today:
If you can afford it: If you make damn sure you do your research; and pick health professionals with solid credibility (sooooo important).

When you find a good skin guy/girl (because you do need to monitor potential sun damage, other health/skin issues etc.) you will notice that they do not try to 'sell you' extra procedures and he/she will say "NO" when you ask for something you don't' really need! If you have 5 kids and you need to tuck your boobs into your belt, there's nothing wrong with a boob-lift. These days breast cancer is not a death sentence and some degree of reconstruction can certainly make you feel like your original self again. But do your homework; even then, surgery is surgery and getting the wrong surgeon can be hell on wheels! In anything you want in life weigh priorities with costs, risks and rewards! When you make well informed decisions you avoid a lot of regrets!

There is nothing wrong with getting a little body modification or help to hold back the years BUT seriously! Use your brain! If the person about to make you beautiful looks like a clown, has lips taking up half their face and desperately needs to eat a muffin OR stopped looking natural 15 procedures ago!!!!!!!!! STOP! (Girls if you're doing it to get a man then don't! Most of the time men don't want it, we do! AND that's ok, but be real!)

There are plenty of professionals out there who can give a little natural looking help BUT cosmetic enhancements WILL NOT dramatically change your life, how you feel about 'you' and your relationships: Plastic surgery is not a substitute for psychotherapy! If your partner doesn't love you now, new boobs or pecks won't fix anything. IF YOU DO IT, DO IT FOR YOU AND HAVE REALISTIC EXPECTATIONS!!!!

Keep it real!

Back to exercise and eating regimes! Pushing yourself is fine as long as you do not put yourself in situations where you are exercising with people who are way out of your league and you start comparing yourself with them… this leads to feeling lousy and giving up. That celeb or athlete you want to be like has to work really hard to keep that body; you certainly can have what they have but you also have to do the work: Pink's money and fame did not make her look hot one year after having her baby! Hard work did! (Of course money for trainers and time etc. certainly help)

IF you must compare… look both ways, back to the people who are not doing as well as you are (yet)…. or just commend yourself for staying in the game AND remember you are doing this for YOU not for anyone else.

IT IS NOT A RACE AND IT IS NOT A
COMPETITION:
IT IS YOUR LIFE!

Necessities of Life!

SUN, FUN

MODERATION

TO DAYDREAM

GOOD FOOD, EXERCISE

AFFECTION, FRIENDSHIP

PHYSICAL SAFETY AND SECURITY

FINANCIAL SECURITY

THE RIGHT TO BE WRONG

BEING LISTENED TO

FEELING HEARD

GUIDANCE

RESPECT

VALIDATION

EXPRESSING FEELINGS: Including Anger

SENSE OF BELONGING

NURTURING

INTIMACY

SEXUAL EXPRESSION

LOYALTY AND TRUST

SENSE OF ACHIEVEMENT

SENSE OF FREEDOM AND INDEPENDENCE

TO FEEL WORTHY

HOPE

NOT NECESSARILY IN THIS ORDER

Engage in confidence building activities; hang with people around whom you feel good!

Getting Active: Activities consist of;

❖ Things you NEED to do

❖ Things you WANT to do

❖ Things you can 'get around to' if and when you feel like it

WHEN YOU DON'T FEEL LIKE DOING MUCH BUT YOU WANT TO FORCE YOURSELF TO DO SOME THINGS!   Often you end up feeling a sense of achievement that you actually got SOMETHING done!

EXERCISE: Plan your day/week or if that's TOO hard start with planning the next few hours: (OK so you don't like 'exercise' but I guarantee there are ways of moving your body that you do enjoy…think about it and make a list.. You may even like putting loud music on and dancing around the house naked! That's also called exercise! Whatever works for you!

BREAK IT UP into:
Pleasure activities… (It is essential to incorporate pleasure/leisure/fun activities into every day). Pushing clients to factor FUN into their lives can be really hard: excuses are usually around time, money and kids… Your choice though; you either want to live long happy and healthy or you don't!

SO!!!!!!!!!!Start NOW! Your first activity is TO DO THIS EXERCISE!

IF YOU WAIT UNTIL YOU FEEL LIKE DOING IT, IT MAY NOT GET DONE! So encourage yourself NOW! Even if you do a little bit of something toward your new improved lifestyle you will start to be proud of yourself and you can build on that….

It is never OK for someone else to nag you! BUT sometimes it is good to nag yourself!

Survival Patterns!

NEGATIVE THOUGHTS ARE ACTIVITY BLOCKERS......

Thoughts such as......

- NO POINT IN TRYING
- NOT GOOD ENOUG
- NOT SMART ENOUGH
- WHAT'S THE POINT
- PROBABLY FAIL ANYWAY
- ETC.,ETC.,ETC.,

SELF DEFEATING FEELINGS AND THOUGHT LEAVE YOU DISCOURAGED. FEELING INADEQUATE, HELPLESS, HOPELESS, AND USELESS!!!

Smokes, Drinks
& all that other stuff!

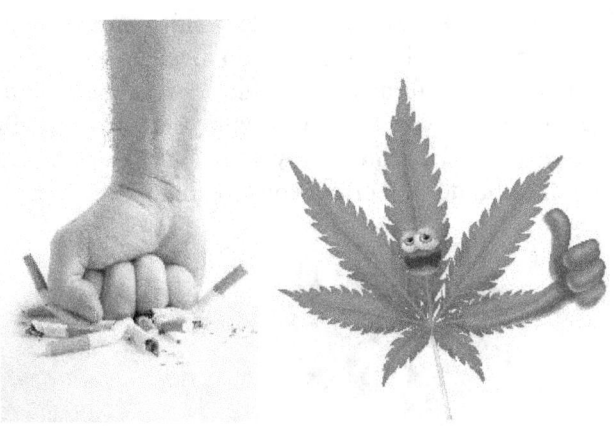

SMOKING: You already know all the warnings! All the horrific outcomes! So simply: It makes you smell disgusting! Going outside and or waving your hands around to magically de-stink the air...Really???? It's in your hair, your skin and your clothes. If you smoke you smell bad: Your skin ages rapidly! At 40 you will look 60!

It is what it is! Your choice.... Unless you actually care about your kids!

IF you have kids, smoking IS probably going to make them smoke too! It also tells them you do not care about them enough to try and stick around longer. TV ads make sure they know what smoking is doing to their parents.

STOP lying to yourself and others!
STOP saying you can't quit! If you want to bad enough you will! Your life is yours to ruin anyway you want BUT if you're a parent then it's not *just* your life! My Quit

Smoking CD on my site works provided you do at some level wish to quit!   If you can't afford $10 for the CD email me I will send it to if you swear to use it!!!!

Hiding your smokes so that people won't nag you only makes them a forbidden fruit: your brain wants something even more if it is a forbidden pleasure. So be honest with the people around you as well as with yourself: you will quit or you won't. But never say you cant.. If the world ran out of cigarettes tomorrow you would not die.

ALCOHOL: If you are a person who can drink X amount and stop! IF you never binge, throw up, have black outs/memory loss, suffer alcohol related regrets and embarrassments! IF you never drive or do stupid dangerous stuff because of alcohol! AND most of all if the answers you gave YOU to all of the above are the truth, the whole truth.... Then fine....... Enjoy!

BUT if the truth is more like this......???

I hear some interesting definitions of "I don't drink....
apparently it can mean:

- ❖ I only drink X (beer/rum, whatever)
- ❖ I only get wasted once a month
- ❖ I am not a heavy drinker
- ❖ I only binge drink
- ❖ I don't think I have a problem
- ❖ No one sees me when I'm plastered

Silly me: I always thought it meant: "I don't drink any
form of alcohol at any time"

Likewise with "I do not have an alcohol problem" this seems to mean:

- ❖ I don't drink before noon
- ❖ I don't drink every day
- ❖ I don't drink out of a bottle in a brown paper bag
- ❖ I don't miss work through my drinking
- ❖ I manage to hide it from others
- ❖ I haven't been arrested
- ❖ The latest one I hear is "wine isn't alcohol!!"
- ❖ I don't think my drinking is excessive even though others might
- ❖ My friends are worse than I am
- ❖ No one sees me when I'm plastered

I could go on but I think you get what I am saying.

You need to get real with yourself!

Don't be a victim Take your life back!

You can do anything if you want it badly enough! Sorry there is not magical fix for alcohol dependence: Only the truth!

FACT FOR QUITTING ALCOHOL:

Your friends may not help; when they see you taking control and making new choices it is like holding a mirror in their face: they may prefer to think being wasted every weekend is fun and they don't want you flaunting reality!

NO you cannot become a social drinker! You may pull it off for a couple of years BUT if alcohol is a problem for you then it's all or nothing, sooner or later it will come out of left field and pull you back down. Alcohol is a very powerful adversary; do not underestimate the power it has over most people! OR just how sneaky it can be!

Quitting is a hard lonely battle, most people will not understand, you will get criticism, you will have people wanting you to drink! GET SUPPORTIVE HELP FROM THE PEOPLE WHO ARE RIGHT FOR YOU!

Do not engage in justifying or explaining your decisions: If necessary lie to these people if that's what it takes to get them off your case! I do not mean lie about the bottle under the bed! I mean tell them you're the designated drive OR you can't drink because you're on medication OR your coke has rum in it! Lying to an annoying drunk is not a crime if it's what you need to do to shut them up!

One client actually got into trouble with a supposedly good friend, because it was the friend's wedding and she pretty much demanded that the client drink at her wedding! (So who has the problem there!!!!!)

GOOD NEWS! You probably will not believe this yet but I promise you that divorcing alcohol does not mean an end to having fun, socializing, getting silly etc. etc.

Once you have lived your new lifestyle for a while you will find you can get just as crazy without alcohol (you may not laugh at some Aussie humor though. I notice for some comedians, their success is dependent on having the audience drunk.) Again, my CD to Quit Alcohol really does work (even with stubborn drinkers)

So Enjoy Moderation in all things Including Moderation:

Live Long Healthy & Happy

Do not buy into the myths of ageing!

Feed your heart as well as your tummy!

Good Sex & Fine Chocolate fix most things!

"The Little Book & CD" series.

Your Child the Little Scientist

The Little Book to Revive Relationships

The Little Book to Annihilate Anxiety

The Little Book to Push Through Pain

The Little Book to Defeat Depression

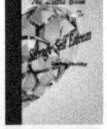

The Little Book to Salvage Self Esteem

The Little Book to be Physically Phabulous

Amazing Abilities of your Magical Mind

CD therapy

 Anxiety

 Alcohol

 Drugs

 Depression

 Smoking

 Self Esteem

 Relationships

 Pain

 Abandonment

 Sleep

 Anger

 Health

 Magical Mind

Bibliography

Albert Ellis (1995)*Clinical Applications of Rational-Emotive Therapy*

Albert Ellis (1995) *Handbook of Cognitive Therapy Techniques*

Elizabeth Hills (2006) Getting in touch with your inner bitch,

Jon Kabat-Zinn, (2008)Full Catastrophe Living

MacKay & Fanning (2002) Self Esteem

Manual J Smith (2000) When I say No I feel Guilty

Michael J Free (1999) Cognitive therapy in groups*: Guidelines and resources in practice*

Rudolph Dreikurs (1985) Happy Children

Sat Chuen Hon, (1999) The Tao of Breath

Illustrations & Photography (2012) Friends 7 Family. Amanda Hockley. Istockphotos.com: Fotolia.

Myke Ashley Cooper: (Page 10) Cartoon used with the permission and generosity of the author.

THE AUTHOR

Denisia Hockley
Clinical Psychologist/Psychotherapist/Author
Dip.Psy.,BA.,BSc.(Hon)Masters Mental Health (Psychotherapy)
Registered AHPRA: (Australia): MAPS Clinical College (Australia)
Member APS (American Pain Society)
Member Association of Independent Authors USA
www.littlebookseries.us
littlebooks2013@gmail.com

Denisia J. Hockley is an Australian Clinical Psychologist: Since 1998 she has worked with everything from general anxiety and depression to victims of trauma and abuse to everyday families struggling with typical life issues as well as those with clinical psychiatric disorders. In 2010 she worked in California specializing in clients with chronic pain issues. As a therapist, she has worked in outback aboriginal settlements, men's correctional facilities, addictions programs and private practice/s. Her style is laidback informal, and solution-focused. As well as CBT, Psycho-education and other general practices she is a qualified psychotherapist and also works with Prof. Leon Petchkovsky with his Neuro feedback clinic. An ex-policewoman, she has had a colorful and diverse career. Denisia's specialties include Complex Post Traumatic Stress Disorder (CPTSD) & Developmental Trauma (non-organic) in adults and adolescents: which result in anxieties, depression, personality disorders, relationship and self-concept difficulties as well as many physiological symptoms including pain and gastrointestinal disorders.

She is most passionate and fascinated by brain science and as she terms it... The Amazing Abilities of our Magical Minds, She has written a number of book including *Your Child the Little Scientist:* Her Little Book Series address every aspect of life, health, happiness, and mental wellbeing and can be obtained as E-Books at www.littlebookseries.us She also has a series of CD therapies covering Sleep/Addiction/Health & Weight/Anxiety/Depression and more: Visit her site for more information on these.